ROMANIA THROUGH THE AGES

A BRIEF HISTORY

By

Martin Miller-Yianni

COPYRIGHT AND CREDITS

Publisher: Martin Miller-Yianni, Yambol, Bulgaria

First Printing Edition 2023

ISBN 978-619-7742-18-3 (Paperback)

A CIP catalogue record for this book is available from:

The National Register of Published Books in Bulgaria
bulevard 'Vasil Levski' 88,
1504 Sofia,
Bulgaria

Cover Photograph (Arco di Trionfo, Bucharest)
By Nicole Baster from Unsplash.com

All Internal photographs and images are courtesy of Wikipedia

TABLE OF CONTENTS

INTRODUCTION

Whether you are a student, a curious traveller, or someone eager to delve into the history of Romania, this book proves to be an invaluable resource. Its well-organised structure and clear presentation facilitate easy navigation through various historical periods and chapters, allowing readers to swiftly locate specific information.

From the ancient Dacian civilisations to contemporary developments, this book comprehensively covers the essential facets of Romania's history. It enables readers to grasp the historical context and cultural heritage of the country. Its concise format makes it an ideal choice for those in search of a quick reference or an introduction to Romania's past.

This book offers a comprehensive overview without compromising on accuracy or depth. It presents information in a readable and accessible British English style, making it an excellent resource for gaining knowledge about Romania's diverse historical foundations.

It's worth noting that some chapters may appear to recap on important events. This is inevitable as era transitions often share events and important figures, which helps reinforce the interconnectedness of Romania's history. Such recapitulations serve as valuable reminders and aids in comprehending the broader historical narrative.

Whether you wish to refresh your knowledge of a specific historical era or develop a general understanding of Romania's past, the book delivers reliable information and serves as an invaluable guide. It immerses readers in the triumphs, challenges, and cultural metamorphoses that have contributed to Romania's identity, offering a fascinating journey through time.

In conclusion, "Romania Through the Ages: A Brief History" is an engaging and informative book that provides a succinct yet comprehensive look at Romania's history. It is an exceptional resource for anyone eager to explore the fascinating story of this nation and gain a deeper appreciation for its rich cultural heritage.

CHAPTER 1 - ROMANIA PREHISTORY

Welcome to our journey through Romania's history, where we'll start at the very beginning, in a time long before written records. This chapter is all about prehistory, a period shrouded in mystery but filled with fascinating discoveries.

Our story begins with an incredible find in Peştera cu Oase[1], or the "Cave with Bones." Here, archaeologists uncovered human remains dating back to roughly 40,000 years ago. These ancient bones belong to some of the first Homo sapiens in Europe. They were the pioneers of their time, and their presence would shape the future of this continent.

As time passed, something remarkable happened in Romania: The Neolithic agricultural revolution. Around the 6th millennium B.C., people from Thessaly arrived, bringing with them the knowledge of farming. This marked a significant turning point as agriculture brought prosperity and stability to the region.

Another exciting discovery took place near a salt spring at Lunca. It's here that we find the earliest evidence of salt production in Europe, a practice that began between the 5th and 4th millennium B.C. Salt became a valuable resource, essential for preserving food and flavouring meals.

---

[1] "Peştera cu Oase" is otherwise known as "Cave with Bones."

Peștera cu Oase

Over time, permanent settlements began to take shape. These early communities grew into what we now call "Proto-Cities," and they were surprisingly large, covering areas larger than 320 hectares (800 acres). They showcase the resourcefulness and organisation of their inhabitants.

In the 3rd millennium B.C., a remarkable culture known as the Cucuteni–Trypillia culture thrived in regions like Muntenia, southeastern Transylvania, and northeastern Moldavia. Their archaeological legacy continues to intrigue researchers and history enthusiasts to this day.

Around 1800 B.C., Romania saw the emergence of fortified settlements. These fortifications tell us about the challenges faced by Bronze Age societies and their determination to protect their homes and communities.

As we step back in time through Romania's history, remember that these early chapters set the stage for the rich network of cultures, events, and innovations that would follow in the centuries and millennia ahead. The people of prehistoric Romania, through their resilience and resourcefulness, left an enduring legacy that still influences the country today.

CHAPTER 2 - ANCIENT DACIA

In the annals of history, the saga of Ancient Dacia unfurls, harking back to a time when the terrain we now recognise as modern-day Romania was home to a world of diverse Thracian tribes. These early settlers brought with them an array of unique cultures and languages, sowing the seeds for the intricate and multifaceted history that would grace this land.

As the 5th century B.C. dawned, the myriad Thracian tribes that roamed this territory gradually coalesced into distinct tribal kingdoms. Two of these, the Getae and Dacae tribes, would emerge as prominent players on this historical stage. By the 1st century B.C., the remarkable King Burebista would succeed in uniting many of these disparate tribes under a single, potent banner.

A momentous juncture in the narrative of Ancient Dacia materialised during 101-102 A.D. when Emperor Trajan embarked on a daring campaign to conquer this territory. This ambitious undertaking, spanning two gruelling Dacian Wars (101-102 A.D. and 105-106 A.D.), culminated in the triumphant annexation of Dacia into the vast embrace of the Roman Empire. The city of Ulpia Traiana Sarmizegetusa, which we now recognise as Hunedoara, was anointed as its illustrious capital.

King Burebista

Under the benevolent sway of Rome, Dacia underwent a profound process of Romanisation. Roman settlers and seasoned veterans were actively encouraged to transplant themselves to Dacia, bringing with them the rich innovative of Roman culture, the Latin tongue, and the administrative acumen that characterised the Empire. Dacia, nestled in the heart of Eastern Europe, metamorphosed into an unassailable bastion of Roman influence.

Dacia's prosperity was inextricably bound to its bountiful mineral resources, with gold, silver, and salt being the jewels in its crown. These precious resources not only adorned its coffers but also endowed it with staggering strategic significance within the sprawling realm of the Roman Empire. The lifeblood of Dacia flowed into the veins of the empire, sustaining its economic vigour.

However, the 3rd century A.D. ushered in a tumultuous era for Dacia as it faced a relentless onslaught of invasions by various barbarian hordes, with the Goths carving their name prominently in the annals of history. The deteriorating security situation forced the Roman Empire to make a fateful decision in 271 A.D. – a withdrawal of its legions from Dacia. This marked the poignant end of Dacia's tenure as a Roman province.

Yet, the spirit of Dacia refused to be extinguished. Even as the Roman legions departed, vestiges of Romanised Dacian communities persevered. The Latin language continued to echo through the ages, weaving its influence into the fabric of local tongues. This cultural and linguistic legacy would play an instrumental role in the forging of the Romanian language and identity, etching an enduring mark on the region's storied history.

Following the Roman withdrawal, Ancient Dacia became a crucible for the great migrations of the era. A multitude of peoples, including the Huns, Visigoths, and Slavs, swept through its lands, reshaping the demographic landscape and further enriching its history.

Today, the legacy of Ancient Dacia continues to be unveiled through the tireless efforts of archaeologists in modern-day Romania. These intrepid explorers unearth a trove of artifacts and ancient settlements from the Dacian and Roman periods, granting us invaluable insights into the material culture and daily existence of Ancient Dacia.

The inaugural chapter of this chronicle has delved deep into the captivating origins of Ancient Dacia. From its diverse Thracian progenitors to the monopoly of Roman conquest and the subsequent influences that reverberated through time, this pivotal epoch marked the birth of a civilisation that would cast an indelible imprint upon the formation of Romania's identity and culture.

CHAPTER 3 - ROMAN PROVINCE

The Roman conquest of Dacia unfolded during the early 2nd century A.D. under the astute leadership of the formidable Roman Emperor Trajan. This ambitious endeavour spanned two major campaigns, the first occurring in 101-102 A.D. and the second in 105-106 A.D. These campaigns were marked by their strategic brilliance and unwavering determination, orchestrated by the resolute Trajan and his formidable legions. On the opposing side, the Dacian King Decebalus emerged as a tenacious adversary, putting up a fierce resistance. Yet, it was ultimately the military prowess and unyielding perseverance of the Roman legions that secured victory, leading to the transformation of Dacia into a Roman province.

Emperor Trajan was the driving force behind the Roman conquest of Dacia. His military acumen and unwavering determination were instrumental in achieving victory. Trajan's leadership left an indelible mark on the history of Dacia and the Roman Empire as a whole.

Decebalus, the Dacian King, emerged as a formidable opponent to Trajan's ambitions. His tenacity and skilful resistance prolonged the conflict, making him a key figure in the Dacian Wars. General Maecenas played a pivotal role in preserving Roman authority and defending the province's frontiers. His military leadership was instrumental in maintaining control and safeguarding the region.

The Romans, under Trajan's command, embarked on extensive infrastructure projects in Dacia, leaving a lasting legacy of engineering prowess. One of the most iconic achievements was Trajan's Bridge, spanning the mighty Danube River, facilitating trade and communication. Notable cities like Ulpia Traiana Sarmizegetusa, serving as the provincial capital, Apulum[2], and Napoca[3] were either established or significantly expanded during this period. These urban centres boasted Roman-style architecture, complete with grand forums, magnificent temples, and splendid bathhouses, showcasing the Romans' commitment to urban development.

The Roman presence ushered in the Latin language and Roman customs to Dacia. Latin swiftly became the official language of the region, and its enduring impact on the Romanian language, which evolved from Vulgar Latin, is unmistakable. Additionally, Roman law and administrative systems were introduced, profoundly influencing governance and jurisprudence in the area.

Dacia's abundant natural resources, including reserves of gold, silver, iron, and salt, were fully exploited under the leadership of figures like Trajan. This resource extraction significantly bolstered the province's economy. Agriculture and trade

---

[2] Apulum is known today as Alba Iulia
[3] Napoca is now known as Cluj-Napoca

flourished, with Dacia emerging as a crucial source of grain for the wider Roman Empire, contributing to the economic prosperity of both the province and the empire as a whole.

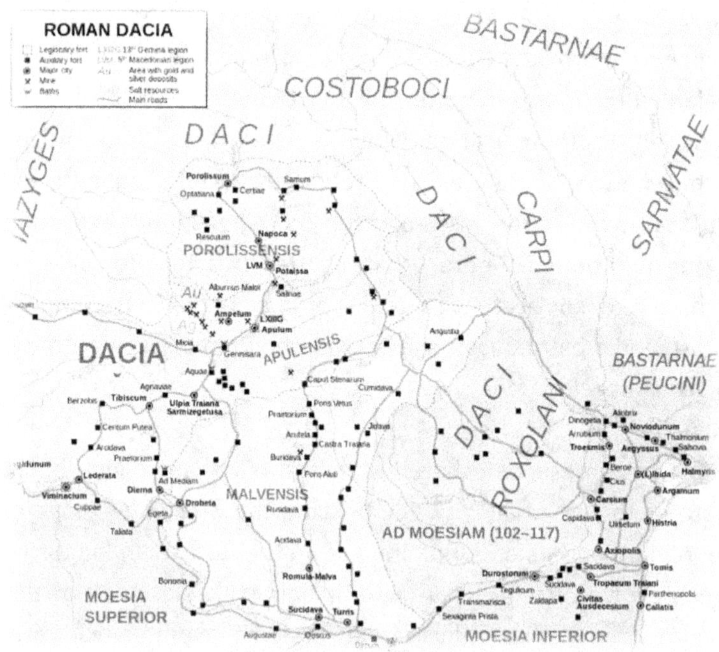

Roman Dacia

Roman religious practices and deities were introduced alongside the persistence of some local gods. Temples devoted to Roman gods and goddesses proliferated, while the cult of Mithras gained traction among the populace, reflecting the syncretic nature of religious beliefs during this period.

To maintain control and safeguard the region, the Romans maintained a substantial military presence in Dacia. Legions such as the XIII Gemina and V Macedonica played pivotal roles in preserving Roman authority and defending the province's frontiers, ensuring the stability of the newly acquired territory.

The Roman presence in Dacia, while remarkable, was not without its challenges. Emperor Aurelian had to contend with recurring barbarian incursions, economic pressures, and political turmoil within the Roman Empire itself, all of which strained the province's stability. In 271 A.D., during the reign of Emperor Aurelian, the Romans took the strategic decision to withdraw from Dacia. This withdrawal marked the end of Roman rule in the region and was motivated by the need to secure the Empire's more defensible borders in the face of external threats.

The Roman legacy endured in the territory that would later become Romania, leaving an indelible mark on its culture and identity. The Latin language and Roman customs, championed by peers like Trajan, played a pivotal role in shaping Romanian culture and language, serving as foundational elements of its rich historical past. Today, Roman ruins, fortifications, and infrastructure remain prominent historical sites in modern Romania, serving as enduring reminders of the profound impact of the Roman period and the influential leaders of the time on the region's history and heritage.

CHAPTER 4 - THE MIGRATION PERIOD AND ROMANIA'S BIRTH

The Migration Period, often referred to as the Barbarian Invasions, stands as a pivotal era in the history of the future Romanian lands. This chapter delves into the intricate details of this transformative period, spanning from the late 4th century A.D. to the 6th century A.D., marked by the fall of the Western Roman Empire.

In 106 A.D., Emperor Trajan's conquest of Dacia established a thriving Roman province known for its abundance of resources, including gold, silver, and fertile terrain, making it a prosperous enclave within the Roman Empire.

During the 3rd century A.D., the Western Roman Empire grappled with internal strife, economic hardships, and mounting external pressures from barbarian tribes. These challenges had a profound impact on Roman governance in Dacia.

Among the earliest migrating groups were the Visigoths, a Germanic tribe. Following the Roman withdrawal from Dacia in 271 A.D. under Emperor Aurelian, the Visigoths crossed the Danube River and began establishing settlements in what is now Romania. Their migration marked the initial shift in the region's demographic composition.

Emperor Aurelian

The Huns, led by the formidable Attila, emerged as a dominant force in Eastern Europe. Their relentless invasions exerted immense pressure on various tribes, compelling them to move further into the Roman Empire, including the territories that would later become Romania.

Simultaneously, the Slavic people embarked on a southward migration into the Carpathian Basin and parts of present-day Romania. Their presence significantly contributed to the ethnogenesis of the Romanian people, as they intermingled with the indigenous Dacian and Roman populations.

With the continued weakening of the Roman Empire, Roman legions had largely departed from Dacia by the early 5th century. This vacuum of power facilitated the more permanent settlement of migratory groups in the region, leading to the emergence of new political entities and settlements that fundamentally reshaped the landscape.

The amalgamation of diverse ethnic groups, including indigenous Dacians, Romans, Visigoths, Huns, and Slavs, played a central role in the formation of the Romanian people. The Latin language, originally spoken by the Romans in Dacia, gradually evolved into the foundation of modern Romanian, retaining its status as a Romance language with notable Slavic and other influences.

The Migration Period left an enduring mark on Romanian culture, language, and identity. It introduced new artistic elements, religious beliefs, folklore, and daily practices. This era also witnessed the spread of Christianity among the various migrating groups, shaping the religious landscape of the region.

The Migration Period drew to a close in the 6th century as migrating groups began to settle and establish their own kingdoms and territories. This marked the transition to the early medieval period in the region, with the emergence of the first medieval Romanian principalities in the centuries that followed.

This chapter provides a comprehensive exploration of the profound and enduring impacts of the Migration Period on the future Romanian lands. It encompasses the end of Roman rule in Dacia, the influx of new ethnic groups, the birth of the Romanian people, and the evolution of the Romanian language. The legacy of this era persists in the rich cultural and linguistic heritage of modern Romania.

CHAPTER 5 - ROMANIAN PRINCIPALITIES EMERGE

In the late 13th century, Wallachia, known as Ţara Românească in Romanian, took shape as a principality under the leadership of the Basarab dynasty, with Basarab I as its esteemed founder. Situated in the southern region of modern-day Romania, Wallachia's strategic location along the lower Danube River made it a coveted and frequently contested territory. During its formative years, Wallachia faced threats from neighbouring entities, including the Kingdom of Hungary and the Golden Horde.

A pivotal moment in Wallachia's history unfolded during the Battle of Rovine in 1395. Under the leadership of Mircea the Elder, the principality successfully repelled an invasion by the Ottoman Empire. This victory not only secured Wallachia's autonomy but also showcased its remarkable ability to withstand external pressures, solidifying its position as a distinct and resilient entity.

Moldavia, known as Moldova in Romanian, emerged as an autonomous principality in the 14th century, with Bogdan I as its founding figure. Located in northeastern Romania, Moldavia faced challenges from various external forces, notably the Golden Horde and the Ottoman Empire. However, it was during the reign of Stephen the Great (Stefan cel Mare) that Moldavia reached its peak.

Stephen the Great

Stephen is celebrated for his military prowess and his unwavering efforts to defend Moldavia from external threats. His reign witnessed Moldavia's territorial expansion, transforming it into a regional power of considerable influence. This period also witnessed remarkable cultural and religious growth, with the Orthodox Christian Church assuming a central role in Moldavian society.

Transylvania, nestled in the northwestern part of contemporary Romania, possessed a distinctive historical narrative due to its diverse ethnic and cultural composition. Initially a part of the Kingdom of Hungary, Transylvania gradually gained a degree of autonomy during the 12th century under the leadership of local Hungarian nobility.

Transylvania's historical landscape was marked by the intricate interplay between Hungarian and Romanian influences, compounded by its proximity to various European powers. The region became a crucial battleground during the Ottoman-Habsburg conflicts and experienced the transformative impact of the Protestant Reformation.

Throughout this epoch, the Romanian principalities faced a series of shared challenges and interactions:

The Ottoman Empire loomed as a significant and enduring menace to these principalities. Ottoman expansionism resulted in numerous confrontations and conflicts, with Wallachia, Moldavia, and Transylvania all grappling with Ottoman incursions and invasions.

The Orthodox Christian Church occupied a central role in the cultural and religious milieu of these principalities. It served as a unifying force for the Romanian populace, preserving their distinctive identity and traditions.

The principalities adhered to a primarily feudal social structure, characterised by rulers, nobility, and peasants. The ruling elites often navigated intricate relationships with neighbouring powers, including Hungary, Poland, and the Ottoman Empire.

In addition to fending off external threats, the principalities occasionally became embroiled in internal conflicts over territorial disputes and spheres of influence. These internal power struggles further moulded the political dynamics of the regions.

While the early Middle Ages bore witness to the autonomy and distinctiveness of these principalities, the 19th century ushered in the commencement of the unification process. In 1859, under the leadership of Alexandru Ioan Cuza, Wallachia and Moldavia merged to form a singular state, the United Principalities of Moldavia and Wallachia, which eventually evolved into modern Romania. In 1881, Carol I was proclaimed King of Romania, formalizing the amalgamation of these regions into a united, cohesive nation.

The emergence and evolution of these principalities during the early Middle Ages laid the bedrock for the modern Romanian nation. Each region contributed its unique historical narrative, culture, and resilience to the broader map of Romanian heritage, fostering a profound sense of unity and shared identity among the Romanian people.

Alexandru Ioan Cuza

CHAPTER 6 - OTTOMAN RULE

In the 14th century, a significant transformation swept through parts of Romania, including Wallachia and Moldavia, as they fell under the dominion of the formidable Ottoman Empire. This period of Ottoman rule, spanning numerous centuries, wrought profound changes upon the political and cultural landscape of the Romanian principalities.

Under the sway of the Ottoman Empire, Wallachia and Moldavia found themselves ensnared in a complex relationship with their Ottoman overlords. The Romanian voivodes, while retaining some semblance of local governance, were obliged to pay tribute to the Ottomans in exchange for a measure of autonomy. However, this tribute system exacted a substantial toll on the principalities. It compelled them to provide both military support and financial resources to the Ottomans, rendering it a burdensome arrangement.

The Ottoman Empire, at the height of its power, presented a dual challenge for Wallachia and Moldavia. On one hand, Ottoman suzerainty offered protection against external threats, particularly the encroachment of neighbouring powers. On the other hand, the tribute and military obligations imposed a significant strain on the Romanian principalities, eroding their financial and political independence.

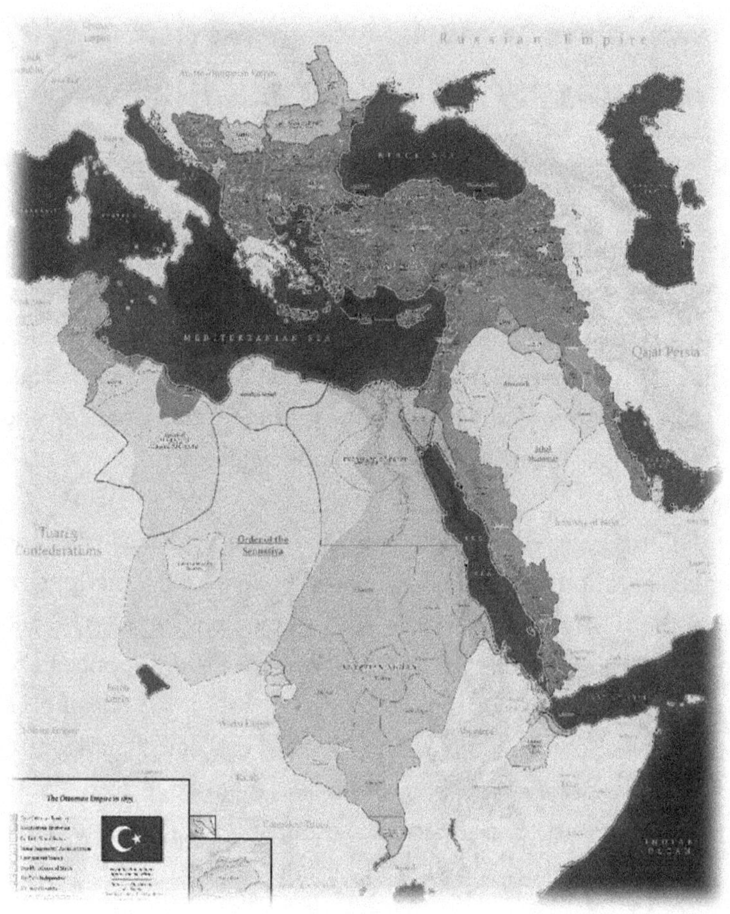

Ottoman Empire 1875

Ottoman rule exerted a profound influence on the cultural and religious fabric of Wallachia and Moldavia. The Ottomans, predominantly adherents of Islam, left an enduring impact on the Christian Orthodox population of these Romanian lands.

This influence engendered a unique fusion of cultures and traditions, resulting in a distinctive cultural syncretism. The Orthodox Church adapted to the Ottoman presence, giving rise to a rich mixture of religious and cultural practices.

Throughout the centuries of Ottoman rule, there were sporadic attempts by Romanian rulers and local nobility to assert greater autonomy. Some voivodes endeavoured to strike a delicate balance between meeting Ottoman demands and preserving Romanian identity and customs. However, these endeavours often encountered resistance from the Ottomans, leading to periods of political turbulence and conflict.

The legacy of Ottoman rule in Wallachia and Moldavia is multifaceted. The tribute system, despite its burdens, left an imprint on the administrative structure of these regions. The experience of centralised rule influenced the governance framework of the later united Romanian state. Moreover, the exposure to Ottoman culture and traditions played a significant role in shaping the diverse cultural mosaic of Romania.

In summary, the era of Ottoman rule in Wallachia and Moldavia, spanning from the 14th to the 19th centuries, stands as a pivotal epoch in Romanian history. It was characterised by a delicate balancing act between preserving local autonomy and meeting the obligations imposed by the Ottoman Empire. This period laid the foundation for the eventual quest for independence and the formation of modern Romania.

CHAPTER 7 - TRANSYLVANIA'S HISTORY

Transylvania, situated in the heart of Eastern Europe, boasts a rich and intricate history, marked by a diverse array of rulers and episodes of self-governance. This comprehensive narrative will delve deeply into the pivotal phases of Transylvania's past, spanning Hungarian and Habsburg rule, while highlighting its evolving relationship with Romania.

Transylvania's historical roots extend to antiquity, when the region was inhabited by a combination of tribes, including the Dacians and Celts. In the 2nd century AD, the Roman Empire extended its dominion over Transylvania, ushering in Latin culture and governance. However, as the Roman Empire faltered in the 4th century, Transylvania faced invasions from various barbarian groups, such as the Huns and Visigoths.

During the early Middle Ages, Transylvania became an integral part of the Kingdom of Hungary, setting the stage for centuries of intertwined destinies. Hungarian rulers established a firm grip over the region, with Transylvania playing a pivotal role in safeguarding the Hungarian kingdom against external threats, including the Mongols and Ottoman Turks.

While Transylvania remained under Hungarian rule, it was also home to a significant Romanian population. This enduring coexistence laid the foundation for a complex relationship between Transylvania and Romania, one that would be shaped by historical events and shifting demographics.

Transylvania's populace was ethnically diverse, comprising substantial Hungarian, Romanian, and German-speaking communities. In the 16th and 17th centuries, Transylvania experienced a period of relative autonomy, often referred to as the "Principality of Transylvania." This era saw a succession of princes, including some of Romanian origin, like Michael the Brave.

This period of autonomy in Transylvania also held significance for its relationship with Romania. It provided opportunities for cultural exchange and the emergence of a distinct Transylvanian identity, while also shaping the aspirations of the Romanian population within the region.

Notably, this period is distinguished by the principle of religious freedom, as exemplified by the Edict of Torda in 1568, which granted religious tolerance to Unitarians, Catholics, Lutherans, and Calvinists. It was a milestone in the history of religious pluralism and had a profound impact on Transylvania's cultural fabric.

The 18th century witnessed Transylvania's integration into the Habsburg Monarchy, a vast empire that left a profound imprint on the region's political and cultural landscape. This era further solidified Transylvania's connection with the wider European context, including its role within the Habsburg Empire.

Michael the Brave (Mihai Viteazu)

The 19th century marked a period of rising nationalism in Transylvania, as well as within the broader region of Romania. The Romanian population began to assert its cultural and national identity, prompting various movements advocating for Romanian rights and self-determination.

This era was crucial in shaping Transylvania's relationship with Romania. The aspirations of the Romanian population within

Transylvania aligned with the broader Romanian national movement, which aimed for the unification of all Romanian-speaking territories, including Transylvania, into a single Romanian state.

The aftermath of World War I brought about significant changes in Transylvania's status. The Treaty of Trianon in 1920 assigned Transylvania to Romania, marking a pivotal moment in Transylvania's relationship with Romania. This decision had profound implications for the region's political landscape and demographics.

Romania's claim to Transylvania was met with mixed reactions from the various ethnic groups residing in the region. While it led to increased cultural and political integration between Transylvania and Romania, it also posed challenges, particularly for the Hungarian minority.

Post-World War II, Transylvania, like the rest of Romania, fell under communist rule under Nicolae Ceauşescu. The collapse of communism in 1989 ushered in political and economic transformations, with Transylvania now part of a democratic Romania.

Today, Transylvania remains an integral part of Romania, elebrated for its cultural diversity and historical significance. Its relationship with Romania continues to evolve, reflecting the complexities of a region that has been shaped by centuries of history, culture, and shared experiences.

CHAPTER 8 - PHANARIOTE RULE IN WALLACHIA AND MOLDAVIA

Through the 18th century, Wallachia and Moldavia, two principalities located in what is now modern-day Romania, experienced a profound and often contentious period of governance under Greek Phanariote rulers. This chapter will take a deep dive into the intricate history of this era, exploring the far-reaching effects of Phanariote rule on these regions and its historical significance in the formation of modern Romania.

Before delving into the era of Phanariote rule, it is crucial to understand the historical context of Wallachia and Moldavia. These territories, despite being under the suzerainty of the Ottoman Empire, had longstanding histories as independent principalities with distinct cultures and identities.

The term "Phanariote" referred to Greek families originating from the Phanar district of Constantinople[4], who held influential positions within the Ottoman Empire. In the 18th century, the Ottoman Empire began appointing Phanariote rulers to govern Wallachia and Moldavia. This marked a significant departure from previous local rulers and set the stage for profound transformations in the region.

---

[4] Constantinople is now modern Istanbul

Phanariote rule brought about both progress and challenges to Wallachia and Moldavia. These Greek rulers, often perceived as outsiders, introduced a series of reforms and administrative changes. While their rule aimed to modernise these principalities, it also sparked controversy and resistance among the local populace.

Under Phanariote rule, efforts were made to centralise power and increase state revenue. These reforms encompassed changes in taxation, the reorganisation of administrative districts, and initiatives to consolidate the authority of the ruling elite. While these measures aimed to strengthen governance, they often resulted in tensions with the local population.

The Phanariote period saw the influence of Greek culture and the Greek Orthodox Church in Wallachia and Moldavia. This influence left a lasting impact on the cultural and religious landscape of these regions, including the promotion of Greek language and traditions.

Phanariote rule was not universally accepted or embraced by the local population. Many locals regarded the Greek Phanariote rulers as foreign oppressors and resented their policies. This discontent frequently erupted into uprisings and revolts against Phanariote authority.

Phanariote rule persisted in Wallachia and Moldavia from the late 17th century into the 19th century. It eventually came to an end due to a combination of factors, including the changing geopolitical landscape in Eastern Europe and the broader decline of the Ottoman Empire.

Ottoman v Phanariotes (Bucharest)

The era of Phanariote rule holds significant importance in the context of Romania's historical development. It marked a period of external influence and political upheaval in Wallachia and Moldavia, both of which played integral roles in the eventual unification of Romania.

The Romanian national movement, which aimed to unite all Romanian-speaking territories into a single state, was gaining momentum during this period. Phanariote rule and the subsequent changes in governance contributed to the evolving sense of Romanian identity and the desire for self-determination.

The Phanariote period left a complex legacy in Wallachia and Moldavia. It brought about both administrative and cultural changes, while also fuelling tensions and resistance. Ultimately, this chapter in history serves as a crucial part of the narrative leading to the formation of modern Romania, highlighting the challenges and aspirations that would shape the nation's future.

the era of Phanariote rule in Wallachia and Moldavia offers a captivating insight into the dynamics of power, governance, and cultural influence in Eastern Europe during the 18th century. Its significance in the context of Romania's history underscores its lasting impact on the region's identity and path to nationhood, making it a pivotal chapter in the annals of Romanian heritage.

CHAPTER 9 - 19TH CENTURY NATIONALISM

The 19th century stands as a pivotal period in the annals of Romania, marked by the fervent emergence of Romanian nationalism and the unyielding struggle for independence from the Ottoman Empire. This chapter embarks upon a detailed exploration of this transformative era, delving into the multifaceted events that laid the groundwork for Romania's modern identity.

To fully comprehend the essence of 19th-century Romanian nationalism, it is imperative to contextualise the historical landscape. Romania, encompassing the principalities of Wallachia and Moldavia, had endured centuries of Ottoman suzerainty. It was an epoch marked by simmering aspirations for self-determination and nationhood, nurtured by the yearning for a distinct Romanian identity.

The 19th century bore witness to the profound awakening of Romanian nationalism—a resolute determination to craft a unique national identity. A cadre of Romanian intellectuals, scholars, and cultural artists played an instrumental role in cultivating this burgeoning sentiment. Literary luminaries such as Mihai Eminescu and Ion Heliade Rădulescu contributed to the reinvigoration of the Romanian language and culture, fostering a burgeoning sense of national pride.

Mihai Eminescu

The earlier Phanariote era, characterised by Greek rulers appointed by the Ottoman Empire, had left an indelible imprint on Wallachia and Moldavia. The Greek influence during this period catalysed the yearning among Romanians for autonomy and a sense of their own destiny.

The 19th century was marked by revolutionary fervor sweeping across Europe, and Romania was not impervious to its influence. The European climate of nationalism and self-determination ignited the aspirations of Romanian intellectuals for liberty and independence. The Revolutions of 1848 reverberated through Romania, further galvanising these aspirations.

A pivotal moment in the quest for Romanian nationhood transpired in 1859, when Alexandru Ioan Cuza was elected as the ruler of both Wallachia and Moldavia. This event, known as the Moldo-Wallachian Union, constituted a significant stride toward unification and independence. While these principalities remained under Ottoman suzerainty, the union laid the groundwork for a single, unified Romania.

The path to complete independence was fraught with challenges. The intricate web of international complexities and the competing interests of neighbouring powers, notably Russia and Austria, complicated Romania's journey towards sovereignty. Nevertheless, the unwavering spirit of Romanian nationalism endured.

The culmination of 19th-century Romanian nationalism came to fruition during the years 1877-1878. Romania seized a momentous opportunity presented by the Russo-Turkish War, declaring its full independence from the Ottoman Empire. Romania actively participated in the war, which culminated in the Treaty of San Stefano and the subsequent Treaty of Berlin.

These treaties affirmed Romania's independence and territorial expansion.

King Carol I

The fervor of 19th-century Romanian nationalism reverberates through the annals of modern Romania. It laid the cornerstone for the unification of Wallachia and Moldavia into the Kingdom of Romania in 1881, under King Carol I. Romania's arduous journey towards statehood, marked by the unwavering struggle for independence, stands as a testament to the indomitable spirit of its people and the enduring power of nationalism.

the 19th century occupies a monumental place in Romanian history, defined by the emergence of Romanian nationalism and the steadfast quest for independence. The legacy of this era endures, etching its indelible mark on Romania's identity as a nation that, against formidable odds, asserted its sovereignty and celebrated its unique cultural heritage.

CHAPTER 10 - THE PIVOTAL STEP TOWARDS UNIFICATION

The mid-19th century unfurled as a period of profound transformation and ferment in Europe, and within the Romanian principalities of Wallachia and Moldavia, it was no exception. This chapter embarks on a comprehensive exploration of the intricate events of 1859, a year that would etch its name into the annals of history as the precursor to the unification of Wallachia and Moldavia, paving the way for the birth of modern Romania.

To fully appreciate the significance of 19th-century Romanian nationalism and the events of 1859, it is imperative to delve into the historical backdrop. These two principalities, Wallachia and Moldavia, while sharing linguistic, cultural, and historical bonds, had long existed as separate entities, both under the suzerainty of the Ottoman Empire. However, beneath this political division simmered a profound yearning for unity and the forging of a distinct Romanian identity.

The 19th century bore witness to the surging tide of nationalism sweeping across Europe, and Romania was no exception. Romanian intellectuals, scholars, and cultural luminaries had, for generations, nurtured the dream of a united Romania. They were inspired by the fervent ideals of self-determination and nationhood. The concept of unification, the establishment of a single Romanian state, began to gather momentum, driven by the shared heritage and destiny of Wallachia and Moldavia.

The pivotal juncture in this quest for unity arrived in 1859 when both Wallachia and Moldavia elected Alexandru Ioan Cuza as their ruler. Cuza, a forward-thinking leader committed to modernisation and administrative reforms, emerged as a beacon of hope for the Romanian people. His election marked the first tangible step towards unification. Cuza's recognition of the common aspirations of the two principalities endeared him to the Romanian populace, earning him their trust and support.

However, the path to unification was fraught with formidable challenges. International complexities loomed large, with neighbouring powers, notably Russia and Austria, harbouring their own designs for the region. Their influence and interests cast a shadow over Romania's aspirations. The determination of the Romanian people and their chosen leader, Cuza, faced adversity head-on, undeterred by the geopolitical intricacies.

The pivotal event that effectively laid the groundwork for the unification of Wallachia and Moldavia was the Moldo-Wallachian Union. This historic step towards unity, albeit with both principalities maintaining distinct administrations, heralded the dawn of a new era for Romania. The union was not only a merger of governance but a symbol of shared dreams and aspirations.

The ultimate culmination of this journey towards unity took place in 1861, catalysed by the election of Alexandru Ioan Cuza. This momentous occasion was met with exuberance and jubilation among the Romanian populace. It represented a profound historical turning point, solidifying the dream of a united Romania.

United Romania 1862

The union of Wallachia and Moldavia under Alexandru Ioan Cuza laid the cornerstone for the Kingdom of Romania, officially declared in 1881 under King Carol I. Romania's arduous journey towards nationhood, marked by the unwavering commitment to unification, stands as a testament to the resilience and determination of its people. The power of a shared vision, of a united Romania, emerged triumphant.

the year 1859 stands as an indelible marker in Romanian history, characterised by the election of Alexandru Ioan Cuza and the unification of Wallachia and Moldavia. This chapter underscores the enduring spirit of Romanian nationalism and the unwavering resolve of its people to forge a united, independent state, ultimately giving birth to modern Romania— a nation woven from the aspirations of a people who yearned to be united under a single banner.

CHAPTER 11 - THE TRIUMPH OF INDEPENDENCE

The late 19th century stands as a pivotal moment in Romanian history, marked by Romania's triumphant journey to independence from the centuries-long suzerainty of the Ottoman Empire. This chapter embarks on an in-depth exploration of the events of 1877-1878, which heralded Romania's remarkable path to sovereignty and international recognition as a sovereign state.

To fully appreciate the significance of Romania's quest for independence, one must consider the historical backdrop. For centuries, Romania had languished under Ottoman rule, with Wallachia and Moldavia existing as distinct principalities. The yearning for autonomy and self-determination had simmered within the Romanian people, fuelled by their shared identity and cultural heritage.

The 19th century witnessed a resurgence of nationalism sweeping across Europe, and Romania was no exception. Romanian intellectuals, patriots, and cultural characters had long harboured the dream of a unified, independent Romania. The spirit of nationalism and a common Romanian identity united the people in their steadfast pursuit of sovereignty.

The turning point arrived with the outbreak of the Russo-Turkish War in 1877. Romania seized this historic opportunity to declare its independence from the Ottoman Empire. The Romanian army, under the leadership of Carol I, actively participated in the war alongside Russian forces, making a substantial contribution to the conflict's outcome.

The Russo-Turkish War culminated in the signing of the Treaty of San Stefano in 1878. This significant treaty recognised Romania's independence from Ottoman rule. Subsequently, the Treaty of Berlin, also in 1878, further affirmed Romania's status as a sovereign state and outlined its territorial borders.

Signing the Treaty of San Stephano 1878

The path to independence was not without its complexities and challenges. Romania had to navigate intricate international diplomacy and negotiations to secure its sovereignty. The great powers of Europe played a pivotal role in recognising Romania as an independent nation.

The attainment of independence in 1877-1878 stands as a defining moment in Romanian history. It marked the conclusion of centuries of Ottoman suzerainty and the dawning of a new era for Romania. The country's journey towards nationhood was officially acknowledged, and it laid the foundation for the modern Romania we know today.

With its independence secured and internationally recognised, Romania embarked on a path of growth and development. The country's territorial borders were expanded, and its institutions were reformed to establish the framework of a modern state. Romania's journey towards nationhood paved the way for its growth as a dynamic and vibrant European nation.

The period of 1877-1878 signifies a defining chapter in Romanian history, characterised by its triumphant quest for independence from the Ottoman Empire. This chapter underscores the indomitable spirit of Romanian nationalism and the unwavering determination of its people to break free from centuries of foreign rule, ultimately forging a path towards a sovereign, unified, and modern Romania that proudly took its place on the world stage.

CHAPTER 12 - THE BIRTH OF THE KINGDOM OF ROMANIA

The latter part of the 19th century emerges as a pivotal epoch in Romanian history, irrevocably defined by Romania's transformative journey into a kingdom in 1881 and the momentous coronation of Carol I as its inaugural monarch. This chapter embarks on a comprehensive exploration of this transformative period, chronicling Romania's journey to becoming a kingdom, its territorial expansions, and the significant acquisition of Transylvania.

To fully grasp the monumental nature of Romania's transition into a kingdom, one must immerse yourself in the historical makeup. Romania had only recently emerged from centuries of Ottoman rule, securing its hard-fought independence in 1878. The nation found itself at a critical juncture, poised to consolidate its gains and assert its rightful place on the international stage.

With independence firmly in hand, Romania turned its gaze towards the institution of monarchy, recognising it as a symbol of unity and stability. The year 1881 witnessed the historic coronation of Carol I, who became the first monarch of the Kingdom of Romania. His ascension to the throne marked the dawning of a transformative era in Romanian history.

The Declaration of the Kingdom of Romania

Romania's path towards nationhood was intricately linked with significant territorial expansions. The acquisition of additional lands played a pivotal role in shaping the nation's geographical borders and cultural identity. This chapter meticulously delves into the intricate details of Romania's territorial gains, meticulously exploring the regions that seamlessly integrated into the heart of the country.

Paramount among these territorial expansions was the coveted acquisition of Transylvania, a region steeped in profound cultural and historical significance. With its substantial Romanian population and rich heritage, Transylvania had long remained an enduring aspiration for Romania. This chapter unravels the complexities surrounding the acquisition of Transylvania, an event that would profoundly reshape the destiny of the nation.

The transition to a kingdom and the relentless pursuit of territorial expansions presented a myriad of challenges. Romania found itself navigating a complex web of internal and external dynamics, engaging in delicate diplomatic negotiations, and astutely assessing the ever-shifting geopolitical realities. Carol I, as the stalwart monarch, played a central and sagacious role in charting Romania's course through these transformative times.

The establishment of the Kingdom of Romania and its consequential territorial expansions indelibly etched their mark on the nation's identity. The legacy of this era, stretching from the illustrious reign of Carol I to the historic acquisition of

Transylvania, resonates in modern Romania. It has been instrumental in shaping Romania as a dynamic and culturally diverse European nation.

the latter part of the 19th century emerges as a momentous period in Romanian history, characterised by the nation's elevation to the status of a kingdom, the coronation of Carol I as its inaugural monarch, and significant territorial expansions, most notably the cherished acquisition of Transylvania. This chapter underscores Romania's inexorable evolution into a sovereign and unified nation, embodying the aspirations, fortitude, and unwavering resolve of its people to forge a brighter, more prosperous future.

CHAPTER 13 - WORLD WAR I

The late 19th and early 20th centuries bore witness to Romania standing at a crossroads, poised to redefine its destiny amidst the tumultuous backdrop of Europe teetering on the brink of World War I. This chapter delves deeply into the intricate web of events that unfolded during the war, altering the course of Romanian history and featuring prominent figures who played pivotal roles in these transformative times.

The chapter commences by immersing the reader in the early 20th century, setting the stage against the complex geopolitical landscape of Europe. Romania, a nascent nation-state, faced the daunting challenge of consolidating its borders and uniting all Romanian-speaking territories under a single national banner. This encompassed regions such as Transylvania, Bukovina, and Bessarabia, inhabited by ethnic Romanians but controlled by neighbouring powers.

In August 1916, Romania took a significant step by officially declaring war on the Central Powers, comprising formidable nations like Germany, Austria-Hungary, Bulgaria, and the Ottoman Empire. Romania's decision to align itself with the Allies stemmed from a fervent desire to realise its territorial aspirations and contribute to the cause of national unity. Key heads at this juncture included King Ferdinand I, who championed Romania's entry into the war, and Prime Minister Ion I. C. Brătianu, a driving force behind the country's foreign policy during this critical period.

The chapter then delves into the early phases of Romania's involvement in the war, highlighting the formidable challenges it encountered as the Central Powers launched a coordinated offensive. Despite initial setbacks, Romania persevered, and its participation on the Eastern Front emerged as a vital theatre of operations. Key strategists such as General Constantin Preza, the Chief of the Romanian General Staff, and General Alexandru Averescu, who led Romanian forces in several key battles, played instrumental roles in bolstering Romania's military efforts.

As the war unfolded, Romania received vital support from the Allies, including Russia, France, and the United Kingdom. The dynamics of the Eastern Front are explored, with a focus on key battles and strategies employed by both sides. This period of Romania's history is portrayed as a time of endurance and resilience in the face of a relentless war machine, with diplomatic efforts led by Nicolae Titulescu, Romania's ambassador in London, also contributing significantly.

A significant turning point in Romania's wartime journey is examined with the Russian Revolution of 1917 and Russia's subsequent withdrawal from the conflict. This development posed new challenges for Romania, but the nation's resilience, coupled with support from the Western Allies, played a pivotal role in its resurgence.

The climax of the chapter revolves around the events of September 1918 when Romanian and Allied forces, guided by battle experts such as General Henri Mathias Berthelot, a French military advisor to Romania, launched a successful counteroffensive, marking a decisive turning point in the war. The Armistice of Compiègne, signed on November 11, 1918, effectively ended hostilities on the Western Front, reshaping the course of history. The role of Romania in these critical events is underscored.

Romanian troops at Mărășești in 1917, during World War I.

The chapter concludes with an exploration of the post-war landscape and Romania's participation in the negotiations that led to the Treaty of Versailles in 1919. This pivotal treaty recognised Romania's territorial gains and its strategic contributions to the Allied cause. Romania emerged from World War I as a significantly expanded nation, with Transylvania,

Bukovina, Bessarabia, and other territories firmly under its control. The chapter highlights the profound impact of Romania's participation in World War I, which not only reshaped its borders but also solidified its national identity and aspirations, with leaders like Ion I. C. Brătianu and King Ferdinand I playing critical roles in shaping Romania's post-war destiny.

CHAPTER 14 - THE INTERWAR PERIOD

The interwar period in Romania unfolds as a multifaceted and pivotal chapter in the nation's history, marked by a dynamic interplay of political, territorial, and societal changes. Romania's journey during this era bore witness to both the zenith of "Greater Romania" and the formidable challenges posed by its diverse populace, as well as external pressures, all of which were significantly influenced by key leaders of the time.

Emerging from the aftermath of World War I, Romania experienced a period of unprecedented territorial expansion. This era, often referred to as "Greater Romania," was underpinned by the visionary leadership of King Ferdinand I, who played a central role in securing significant territorial gains, uniting many Romanian-speaking regions under the nation's flag. The concept of "Greater Romania" encapsulated the nation's territorial ambition and the success it achieved, with King Ferdinand I being a symbol of this achievement.

Amidst the celebration of territorial accomplishments, Romania confronted the intricate task of managing its internal diversity. The nation was home to a mosaic of ethnic groups, each with its own cultural, linguistic, and political aspirations. Prominent politicians such as Prime Minister Ion I. C. Brătianu and Octavian

Goga, leader of the far-right National Christian Party, grappled with the political complexities arising from this diversity, including the rise of nationalist sentiments and the emergence of fascist ideologies.

The interwar political arena in Romania was marked by a delicate balancing act, and figures like Corneliu Zelea Codreanu, founder of the Iron Guard, a far-right and antisemitic movement, played a significant role in shaping the nation's course. The ascendance of nationalism and the emergence of fascist ideologies are explored within the context of their impact on Romanian society, with Codreanu becoming a charismatic and controversial figure.

Romania's strategic location placed it at the heart of a volatile Balkan and Eastern European region. The chapter unravels the external pressures and territorial disputes that confronted Romania, with King Carol II, who succeeded King Ferdinand I, navigating the contentious issue of Bessarabia, a source of protracted tension with the Soviet Union, with a deft hand. The intricate dance of diplomacy and foreign policy is unveiled, with Carol II's decisions significantly shaping Romania's external relations.

Romania underwent remarkable economic transformations during the interwar years. High profile Influencers like Grigore Gheorghiu-Dej, a communist leader in his early political career, played a role in the nation's industrial and economic progress. The nation's industrialisation and modernisation were notable achievements, driven by leaders who recognised the need to transform an agrarian society into an industrially oriented one. The chapter explores these economic strides while also shedding light on the challenges posed by growing economic disparities and social inequalities.

The chapter culminates in an examination of the profound impact of the Great Depression. The global economic crisis reverberated through Romania, leading to economic hardships that, in turn, had cascading political and social consequences. Political guiders like Alexandru Vaida-Voevod, who served as Prime Minister during this tumultuous period, grappled with the economic and social fallout of the Great Depression. The economic crisis ushered in political changes, increased social unrest, and added another layer of complexity to Romania's interwar period.

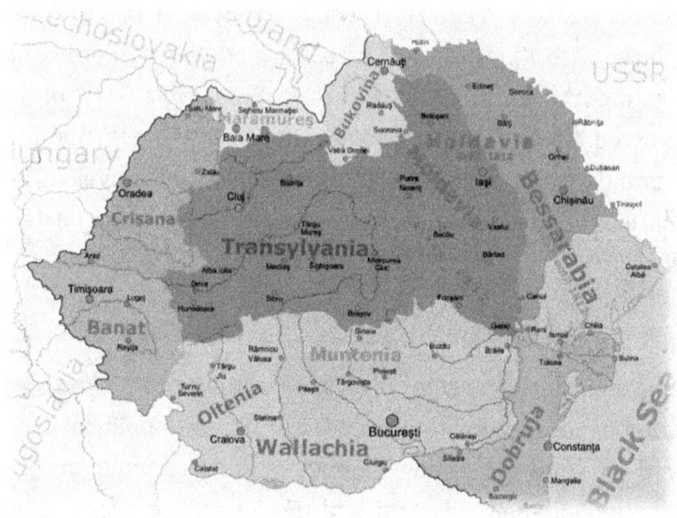

Kingdom of Romania 1918-1940

In summary, this chapter provides an immersive mapping of Romania's interwar period. It intricately weaves together the narrative of "Greater Romania" with the complexities of managing a diverse populace and navigating intricate external relationships, all of which were significantly influenced by key figures of the time, including monarchs, political leaders, and ideological movements. The political, economic, and social transformations that characterised this epoch laid the groundwork for Romania's future, as it stood poised to confront the uncertainties of the 20th century with resilience and adaptability.

CHAPTER 15 - WORLD WAR II

World War II thrust Romania into a maelstrom of unparalleled complexity, and this chapter plunges into the tumultuous period when the nation's destiny was intricately woven into a web of alliances, significant territorial losses, and dramatic realignments. Throughout this chapter, we shall illuminate the influential heads who played pivotal roles in shaping Romania's course during World War II.

As World War II ominously loomed on the horizon, Romania, led by King Carol II, stood at a pivotal crossroads. The nation initially aligned itself with the Axis Powers, a strategic decision driven by territorial ambitions and a fervent desire to reclaim lost territories. This alignment was orchestrated by Marshal Ion Antonescu, who served as Prime Minister and later as Conducător[5] during this period. The diplomatic efforts to forge these ties with Nazi Germany were led by Foreign Minister Mihai Antonescu.

Romania's territorial ambitions focused on regions like Bessarabia, Northern Bukovina, and Transylvania, all of which had been lost following World War I. However, these aspirations exacted a heavy price. In 1940, under intense pressure from Nazi Germany and the Soviet Union, Romania

---

[5] "Conducător" is translated to mean "Leader"

was compelled to cede Bessarabia and Northern Bukovina to the Soviets and Northern Transylvania to Hungary. These events significantly altered the nation's map and were marked by the efforts of key political figures like Premier Gheorghe Grigore Gafencu and the diplomat Grigore Niculescu-Buzești.

Romania's alignment with the Axis Powers came at a considerable cost. The nation became embroiled in the Eastern Front, participating in the invasion of the Soviet Union in 1941. Yet, as the tide of war shifted, Romania faced a momentous decision. In 1944, King Michael I, a young and courageous monarch, orchestrated a daring coup, toppling the pro-German government. This bold move, supported by politicians Nicolae Rădescu, realigned Romania's allegiance towards the Allied Powers, ushering in a dramatic shift in the nation's trajectory.

Romania's shift towards the Allies bore profound consequences. The Red Army, now an ally, rapidly occupied Romanian territory, resulting in the loss of Southern Dobruja and Northern Transylvania. Romania's wartime experience was marred by extensive suffering, including bombings, occupation, and political upheaval.

As World War II drew to a close, Romania played a significant role in the negotiations that led to the Treaty of Paris in 1947. This pivotal treaty, shaped by the evolving geopolitical landscape and the interests of major Allied Powers, formalised Romania's territorial losses and solidified its new boundaries. Prominent leaders like Gheorghe Tătărescu, Romania's Foreign

Minister during this period, were instrumental in representing the nation's interests during these complex negotiations.

King Michael I

In this section, we encapsulate Romania's intricate history through World War II, providing detailed insights into the influential figures who steered the nation's destiny. It chronicles the nation's initial alignment with the Axis Powers, its territorial aspirations and losses, and the momentous political realignment that reshaped its post-war trajectory. For Romania, World War II represented a period of unparalleled complexity and transformation, laying the groundwork for its role in the emerging Cold War era under the guidance of leaders like King Michael I and other key politicians were vital in this turbulent era of history.

CHAPTER 16 - THE COMMUNIST ERA

After the tumultuous conclusion of World War II, Romania found itself at a crossroads, embarking on a transformative journey under communist rule, a period spanning over four decades and culminating in the historic 1989 revolution. This comprehensive chapter explores Romania's turbulent communist era and the influential figures who shaped it.

Following World War II, Romania underwent a seismic political shift. Soviet forces occupied the country, and the monarchy was abolished. In 1947, King Michael I was compelled to abdicate, ushering in the ascent of communist forces to power. Petru Groza, a communist sympathiser and significant figure during this transitional period, became the Prime Minister, marking the inception of Romania's communist era.

Nicolae Ceaușescu, a devoted adherent of the Romanian Communist Party (PCR), emerged as a formidable figure within the party hierarchy. In 1965, he assumed the pivotal role of General Secretary of the PCR. Under his leadership, Romania embarked on a distinct path, diverging from Soviet influence. Ceaușescu championed a policy of national communism, aiming to assert Romania's autonomy within the Eastern Bloc, with an emphasis on nationalism alongside communist principles.

Petru Groza

One of the most striking facets of Ceaușescu's rule was the fervent cult of personality cultivated around him. His omnipresent image adorned the nation's public spaces, and his authority was virtually unassailable. The regime propagated the narrative of Ceaușescu as the beloved "Conducător" (leader) and "Genius of the Carpathians," while dissenting voices were ruthlessly silenced.

Ceaușescu's economic policies, while aimed at reducing Romania's foreign debt, imposed severe austerity measures on the population. The regime embarked on a grandiose program of industrialisation and urbanisation, including the infamous destruction of historic Bucharest neighbourhoods to make way for structures like the People's Palace. However, these ambitions came at a significant human cost, as food and energy shortages became common place, and the standard of living deteriorated for ordinary Romanians.

Nicolae Ceauşescu

The Securitate, Romania's formidable secret police, played a central role in maintaining the iron grip of the Ceaușescu regime. Employing extensive surveillance, intimidation, and brutality, this feared organisation quashed dissent, monitored citizens' activities, and instilled a climate of fear and paranoia.

Ceaușescu's foreign policy stance was marked by notable independence. He sought diplomatic relations with both the United States and the Soviet Union while advocating for a "multilateral foreign policy." This strategy aimed to elevate Romania's international stature while maintaining an unconventional, non-aligned position within the Eastern Bloc.
The late 1980s witnessed mounting discontent with Ceaușescu's oppressive regime. Frustrations over food shortages, censorship, and human rights abuses culminated in protests that rocked the nation. The revolution began in Timișoara in December 1989 when protests against the eviction of a dissident minister spiralled into a nationwide uprising. Ceaușescu's attempts to quell the revolt failed, leading to his flight from Bucharest amidst escalating opposition.

The watershed moment of the Romanian communist era arrived on December 25, 1989, when Nicolae and Elena Ceaușescu were captured, subjected to a hasty trial, and subsequently executed by firing squad. Their fall marked the culmination of the people's desire for freedom and democracy. Romania embarked on an arduous path towards political pluralism, market-oriented reforms, and the dismantling of the oppressive structures of the past.

In summary, Romania's communist era, dominated by Nicolae Ceaușescu's rule, was characterised by authoritarianism, economic hardship, and pervasive repression. The December 1989 Revolution, with its dramatic overthrow of the Ceaușescu regime, was a pivotal moment that ushered in a new chapter in Romania's history, setting the stage for a transition to democracy and a more open society, all of which was significantly influenced by politicians Petru Groza, Nicolae Ceaușescu, and the people who took to the streets in protest.

CHAPTER 17 - THE REVOLUTION OF 1989

The year 1989 is etched in the annals of Romanian history as a watershed moment, witnessing a seismic revolution that dismantled the communist regime and culminated in the execution of Nicolae Ceaușescu. This chapter embarks on a detailed exploration of the multifaceted events and intricate dynamics that shaped the Revolution of 1989 in Romania, highlighting the influential figures who played pivotal roles.

Throughout the 1980s, Romania simmered with a potent mixture of frustration and resentment, ignited by the iron-fisted rule of Nicolae Ceaușescu and the repressive policies of the Romanian Communist Party (PCR). During this period political influencers included Nicolae Ceaușescu himself, the autocratic leader who had held power for decades, and high-ranking members of the PCR, such as Nicolae's wife, Elena Ceaușescu, who wielded considerable influence within the regime.

Grievances among the Romanian populace ranged from acute economic hardships and food shortages to all-pervasive censorship and the ruthless suppression of dissent. The collective disillusionment had reached a critical tipping point, setting the stage for a revolution.

The 1989 Revolution - Bucharest

The spark for the revolution ignited in the western city of Timișoara in December 1989. It began as a protest in response to the impending eviction of László Tőkés, an ethnic Hungarian pastor who had become a vocal critic of the regime. What commenced as a localised outcry rapidly snowballed into a nationwide uprising, fuelled by profound discontent with Ceaușescu's rule. László Tőkés a leading politician and other early protesters became symbols of the burgeoning resistance.

The reverberations of the Timişoara uprising rippled across Romania, sparking a wave of protests in cities and towns nationwide. Citizens from all walks of life took to the streets, united in their demand for an end to the repressive regime and the resignation of Ceauşescu and his inner circle. The revolution was notable for its grassroots nature, with ordinary Romanians propelling the momentum for change.

In a desperate bid to suppress the escalating unrest, Nicolae Ceauşescu delivered a televised address to the nation from the balcony of the Central Committee building in Bucharest on December 21, 1989. However, the crowd's response was far from the expected support; they responded with boos and jeers. Realizing the gravity of the situation, Ceauşescu and his wife, Elena, hastily fled the capital by helicopter, leaving a power vacuum in their wake.

With Ceauşescu's departure, an interim government led by Ion Iliescu, a former high-ranking member of the Communist Party who had fallen out of favour with Ceauşescu, assumed control. The new authorities acted swiftly to dismantle the remnants of the old regime, including the disbandment of the Securitate, the dreaded secret police, and the implementation of crucial political reforms.

Events took an even more dramatic turn when Nicolae and Elena Ceauşescu were apprehended by the authorities on December 22, 1989, in the city of Târgovişte. Their subsequent trial proceeded with remarkable speed, during which they faced charges of crimes against the Romanian people. On December

25, 1989, the Ceaușescus met their fate before a firing squad, an event that sent shockwaves through the nation and the world.

Following the execution of Ceaușescu, Romania entered a tumultuous period of transition, marked by figures like Ion Iliescu, who played a significant role in the country's political evolution. The nation embarked on a journey of political and economic transformation, transitioning from a communist state to a fledgling democracy. However, the transition was beset with challenges, including economic hardships and political turbulence.

The Revolution of 1989 in Romania left an indelible mark on the nation's history. It serves as a testament to the power of popular will and the unwavering desire of the Romanian people for freedom and democracy. While it marked the end of the communist regime, the aftermath presented formidable challenges as Romania grappled with the complexities of forging a new, democratic future.

In summary, the Revolution of 1989 in Romania was a profoundly significant and intricate episode in the nation's history, with key political personalities like Nicolae Ceaușescu, Elena Ceaușescu, László Tőkés, and Ion Iliescu leaving indelible marks on this pivotal moment that symbolised the resilience and determination of the Romanian people in their pursuit of liberty and democratic governance.

CHAPTER 18 - THE POST-COMMUNIST TRANSITION

The 1990s witnessed Romania undergoing a profound and intricate transformation, embarking on the challenging path of transitioning from a decades-long communist regime to a fledgling democracy and a market-oriented economy. This chapter delves into the intricate details of Romania's post-communist transition, a period marked by a myriad of political, economic, and social challenges that would come to define the nation's trajectory during this critical era, including the influential figures who shaped it.

The fall of communism ushered in a newfound sense of political freedom and expression in Romania. The early 1990s saw the emergence of political parties and the nation's inaugural democratic elections in 1990, culminating in the election of Ion Iliescu as president. However, this era was characterised by a fragmented political landscape, with a multitude of parties and ever-shifting alliances, creating a volatile political climate.

The transition towards a market-oriented economy stood as a central pillar of Romania's post-communist transformation. This multifaceted process encompassed the privatisation of state-owned enterprises, economic liberalisation, and integration into the global market. During this economic transition, key influencers included leaders like Theodor Stolojan, who served as Prime Minister and played a significant role in implementing economic reforms.

While these reforms held the promise of economic prosperity, they also brought about significant hardships, including widespread unemployment and rampant inflation, which challenged the resilience of Romanian society. Leaders like Adrian Năstase, who later became Prime Minister, were instrumental in shaping economic policies during this period.

The economic difficulties and uncertainties of the post-communist era triggered social discontent and protests. Romanians voiced their grievances against the reform policies, leading to episodes of civil unrest and strikes. The government had to navigate the delicate balance between the imperatives of economic reform and the pressing needs and expectations of its citizens.

The transition to democracy necessitated the establishment of a robust democratic framework. This included ensuring the rule of law, safeguarding human rights, and building democratic institutions. Crafting a new constitution and reshaping the nation's political culture were complex tasks that demanded careful consideration and political dialogue.

During this period, Romania actively pursued European integration, with figures like President Emil Constantinescu actively championing the nation's bid for European Union (EU) membership. Romania's commitment to aligning its political, economic, and legal systems with EU standards and norms represented a significant step towards broader European cooperation.

Romania grappled with the legacy of its communist past, including addressing human rights abuses and the crimes of the Securitate, the feared secret police. Lustration efforts aimed at holding those responsible for communist-era atrocities accountable, making it a challenging and sensitive process that demanded careful consideration.

As the 1990s drew to a close, Romania had made significant progress in its post-communist transition. Multiple democratic elections had taken place, and the nation had established a market-oriented economy. Progress towards European integration continued. However, significant challenges remained, including corruption, economic disparities, and the ongoing need for democratic consolidation.

The post-communist transition in Romania during the 1990s represented a complex and tumultuous epoch, shaping the nation's contemporary history. It was a period of experimentation, adaptation, and transformation as Romania sought to define its identity in a new era. The legacy of this critical period continues to resonate in Romania's political, economic, and social landscape as the nation advances into the 21st century.

Romania's post-communist transition in the 1990s was a complex and transformative journey, marked by political evolution, economic challenges, and the pursuit of European integration, all had a profound influence, especially Ion Iliescu, Theodor Stolojan, Adrian Năstase, Emil Constantinescu, and many others who played instrumental roles in shaping Romania's path during this crucial era.

CHAPTER 19 - INTEGRATION INTO WESTERN INSTITUTIONS

The early 21st century marked a transformative period in Romania's history, characterised by the nation's determined efforts to integrate into two of the most prominent Western institutions: the North Atlantic Treaty Organisation (NATO) and the European Union (EU). This chapter provides a comprehensive exploration of Romania's intricate journey towards NATO membership in 2004 and its subsequent accession to the EU in 2007, outlining the profound impact of these milestones on the nation, with a focus on the influential figures who had a vital role during this period.

Romania's quest to join NATO was driven by a strategic imperative. The nation sought the security guarantees, collective defence mechanisms, and alignment with Western values that NATO membership could provide. President Ion Iliescu and Prime Minister Adrian Năstase played pivotal roles in spearheading Romania's efforts to meet NATO's stringent criteria, overseeing sweeping reforms, particularly in its armed forces.

Romanian Troops in Afghanistan as part of NATO

Romania's relentless pursuit of NATO membership culminated in a historic moment on March 29, 2004, when the nation officially became a member of the alliance. This achievement symbolised Romania's unwavering commitment to collective defence, its alignment with Western security interests, and its readiness to contribute to NATO's missions worldwide. Traian Băsescu, who later served as President, were instrumental in shaping Romania's role within NATO.

Concurrently, Romania set its sights on EU membership, viewing it as a transformative goal that would catalyse economic development, democratic consolidation, and enhanced regional cooperation. Leaders like Prime Minister Victor Ciorbea and later President Emil Constantinescu led the nation through extensive legislative, institutional, and structural reforms, aligning its policies, laws, and institutions with EU standards and regulations.

On January 1, 2007, Romania achieved another historic milestone was official, namely joining the European Union (EU). This marked a momentous chapter in Romania's evolution as it became a full-fledged EU member state. EU membership opened doors to economic opportunities, political influence, and intensified cooperation with fellow European nations. It was not just a testament to Romania's dedication to democratic values but also an affirmation of its European identity. Prime Minister Călin Popescu-Tăriceanu were crucial in navigating Romania's early years as an EU member.

The road to EU membership was not without its challenges. Romania had to grapple with issues such as corruption, judicial reform, and the effective implementation of EU legislation. However, the benefits were substantial. EU accession granted Romania access to the single European market, structural funds for development, and a platform to actively participate in shaping European policies, enhancing the nation's economic and political standing.

Romania's dual membership in NATO and the EU created synergies that bolstered its position on the international stage. The nation became an integral part of Western security architecture, contributing to peacekeeping missions, security cooperation, and alliance-wide initiatives within NATO. Simultaneously, Romania engaged in EU policymaking, economic development, and regional diplomacy, harnessing the benefits of both memberships to promote its national interests.

Romania's accession to NATO and the EU marked the commencement of an ongoing journey rather than the culmination. The nation continued to work tirelessly to strengthen democratic institutions, combat corruption, and address socio-economic disparities. Romania's active participation in both NATO and the EU affirmed its commitment to the values of these institutions and its determination to play a constructive role in regional and global affairs.

Romania's successful integration into Western institutions held broader implications for the entire region of Eastern Europe. It served as a compelling example that countries with communist legacies could successfully transition into thriving democracies and full-fledged members of the Euro-Atlantic community. Romania's experience offered inspiration and guidance for other nations on a similar path, underlining the transformative power of Euro-Atlantic integration in Eastern Europe.

On reflection, Romania's accession to NATO in 2004 and the European Union in 2007 were watershed moments in the nation's history, significantly influenced by important figures such as Ion Iliescu, Adrian Năstase, Traian Băsescu, Victor Ciorbea, Emil Constantinescu, and Călin Popescu-Tăriceanu, among others. These achievements were the culmination of years of painstaking reforms, reflecting Romania's unwavering commitment to Western values, security, and economic prosperity. Romania's dual membership in these institutions continues to shape its role on the global stage, illustrating the profound impact of Euro-Atlantic integration on Eastern European nations.

Romania Joined the EU in 2007

CHAPTER 20 - INTO THE 21ST CENTURY

The 21st century has ushered in a dynamic and transformative period in Romania's history, where the nation continues to evolve politically, economically, and culturally as a central European player. This chapter offers an in-depth exploration of Contemporary Romania, highlighting the numerous challenges and opportunities that have shaped the country's trajectory in this new millennium, along with the influential figures who were instrumentally vital during this time.

Romania's political landscape in the 21st century has witnessed significant strides towards democratic maturation. Presidents Traian Băsescu and Klaus Iohannis have contributed substantially to the nation's democratic consolidation. Romania has conducted multiple rounds of free and fair elections, solidifying its commitment to democratic governance. A vibrant civil society, led by individuals like activist and politician Monica Macovei, has emerged, actively participating in political discourse, advocating for human rights, and holding those in power accountable.

The Romanian economy has experienced noteworthy growth and transformation in the 21st century. Prime Ministers Adrian Năstase, Călin Popescu-Tăriceanu, and Ludovic Orban have been innovative in implementing economic reforms. The nation has successfully transitioned into a market-oriented economy, attracting foreign investment and nurturing a burgeoning entrepreneurial spirit. However, economic challenges persist, including income inequality, corruption, and the imperative for further structural reforms to ensure sustainable growth.

Ludovic Orban

Romania's accession to the European Union in 2007 marked a watershed moment. As a full-fledged EU member state, Romania actively engages in EU policymaking, benefiting from access to the single European market and structural funds for development. Prime Minister Dacian Cioloş and President Iohannis have played pivotal roles in shaping Romania's position within the EU, advocating for reform and fostering cooperation.

Romania's commitment to ensuring security in the Euro-Atlantic region remains resolute. As a member of NATO since 2004, the nation plays an active role in alliance-wide efforts to address contemporary security challenges. These include countering terrorism, cybersecurity threats, and contributing to NATO's collective defence posture. Romania's strategic location on the eastern flank, recognised by leaders like President Iohannis, adds to its significance in regional security dynamics.

Romania continues to celebrate its rich cultural diversity and heritage. Artistic talents like writer Mircea Cărtărescu and director Cristian Mungiu have contributed to the nation's cultural vitality. Cultural events, festivals, and the preservation of historical sites contribute to Romania's vibrant cultural identity, which remains an integral part of national life.

Romania faces an array of challenges in the 21st century. Prime Ministers Victor Ponta and President Iohannis have worked to address corruption, ensure equitable economic development across regions, and strengthen vital sectors such as healthcare and education. The nation also grapples with demographic challenges, including emigration of its workforce, necessitating long-term planning and policies to sustain economic growth and social stability.

Author - Mircea Cărtărescu

Romania's commitment to European integration remains unwavering. The nation actively participates in EU projects and regional cooperation initiatives, fostering stability and security in Southeastern Europe. Romania's role in the Black Sea region has gained prominence in the context of wider European security considerations. The nation also engages in global diplomacy, contributing to international peacekeeping missions and humanitarian efforts.

Contemporary Romania stands at the crossroads of its rich history and the dynamic challenges and opportunities of the 21st century. The nation's continued evolution is a testament to its resilience and determination to navigate the complexities of a rapidly changing world. Romania embraces its role as a European player while staying true to its European identity and democratic values.

Romania in the 21st century is a nation in flux, led by influential leaders like Presidents Traian Băsescu, Klaus Iohannis, Prime Ministers Adrian Năstase, Călin Popescu-Tăriceanu, Ludovic Orban, Dacian Cioloș, and Victor Ponta, as well as activists and cultural icons like Monica Macovei, Mircea Cărtărescu, and Cristian Mungiu. It embraces its role as a pivotal player in Europe and the world, continuing to shape its path with a vision of the future rooted in its rich cultural heritage and historical legacy, as it strives to meet the challenges and seize the opportunities of the modern era.

CHAPTER 21 - THE FUTURE

As Romania stands at the threshold of the future, the nation is poised to embark on a journey filled with promise and potential. In this chapter, we delve into the myriad possibilities and challenges that may define Romania's trajectory in the years to come. Drawing inspiration from its rich past, we paint a vivid picture of the nation's future.

Turning our gaze ahead, Romania envisions economic prosperity underpinned by innovation and adaptability. Building on its historical strengths, including a skilled workforce and strategic location, the nation is poised to propel economic growth into new horizons. Embracing cutting-edge technology and nurturing a culture of innovation, Romania can position itself as a dynamic player in global industries. Sustainable development practices, rooted in a history of resourcefulness, will lay the foundation for enduring economic stability.

Looking forward, Romania's historical experience of navigating complex geopolitical landscapes will guide its future regional leadership. The nation seeks to actively engage with neighbouring countries, drawing upon its history of diplomacy and cross-cultural interaction to foster stability, cooperation, and economic integration in Southeastern Europe. Romania's unwavering commitment to European integration, forged through decades of reform, will continue to be a driving force, solidifying its position as an influential EU member and shaping the destiny of the continent.

Romania remains steadfast in its commitment to strengthening democratic institutions and upholding the rule of law in the future. Building upon a historical quest for democratic ideals, the nation's efforts to combat corruption, enhance judicial independence, and ensure transparency will be pivotal for its democratic consolidation. Drawing inspiration from its resilient history, Romania's citizens will continue to play a vital role in shaping the country's political landscape, safeguarding the values of democracy and the rule of law.

As Romania charts its path in the years ahead, the nation recognises the critical importance of education and talent retention. By investing in high-quality education, Romania aims to cultivate a skilled and innovative workforce, leveraging its historical appreciation for knowledge. Strategies that encourage talent retention within the country, counteracting the effects of emigration, will be paramount for sustained growth and development, building upon the nation's historical adaptability and resourcefulness.

Romania's commitment to sustainable development and environmental stewardship is deeply rooted in its historical connection to its natural landscapes. As the nation journeying forward, it will work towards reducing carbon emissions, preserving its biodiversity, and harnessing renewable energy sources. Embracing green technologies and sustainable practices, inspired by a history of environmental awareness, will allow Romania to play a pivotal role in global efforts to combat climate change.

Romania's rich cultural heritage and identity, shaped by centuries of diverse influences, continue to be a source of inspiration as the nation ventures into the future. Preserving historical sites, promoting cultural diversity, and supporting the arts remain essential components of the nation's character. Cultural diplomacy, rooted in a history of cross-cultural exchanges, will enhance Romania's global presence and strengthen its bonds with other nations, contributing to global cultural exchange.

Romania's historical experience of engaging with diverse cultures and regions positions it to be an active participant in global diplomacy as it looks ahead. The nation can continue to contribute to international peacekeeping missions, humanitarian efforts, and diplomatic initiatives. By building partnerships and alliances, drawing from its history of bridge-building, Romania can wield influence in international discourse and contribute to global stability.

As the time step on, Romania acknowledges that challenges will inevitably arise, as they have throughout its history. However, the nation's historical journey of resilience, marked by the ability to overcome obstacles and adapt to changing circumstances, serves as a wellspring of strength. Romania draws upon its past experiences and lessons, informed by centuries of trials and triumphs, to navigate future challenges with determination and adaptability.

Bucharest – Romania's Capital

In envisioning its future, Romania aspires to become a prosperous, democratic, and influential nation in the heart of Europe. By building upon historical strengths, fostering economic growth, nurturing talent, preserving its cultural heritage, and actively engaging in global affairs, Romania's future holds the promise of a dynamic and vibrant nation. It embodies the spirit of its historical journey, contributing to a better world for generations to come.

Romania's future unfolds against the backdrop of its rich historical makeup, where the nation's past achievements and challenges provide a compass for its journey ahead. As Romania steps into the unknown terrain of the future, it does so with a sense of optimism and purpose, rooted in its enduring historical legacy. The nation's path forward holds the promise of a dynamic and influential player on the global stage, reflecting its historical resilience and commitment to progress and democracy. Romania's future is a testament to the enduring spirit of a nation with a history that spans centuries, poised to shape its destiny in the 21st century and beyond.

RULERS AND LEADERS OF PRE-MODERN ROMANIA

Ruler/Leader	Dates	Notes
Michael the Brave (Mihai Viteazu)	1593-1601	Significant for his attempt to unite the three principalities of Wallachia, Moldavia, and Transylvania.
Basarab, Matei	1632-1654	Aimed to strengthen Wallachia's autonomy and administration, with efforts to modernize its infrastructure and institutions.
Ștefan, Gheorghe	1654-1658	Ruled Wallachia during a period of political instability and conflict within the principality.
Lupu, Vasile	1659-1661	Served as the voivode of Moldavia and contributed to its cultural and economic development.
Basarab, Matei (Second reign)	1661-1665	Returned to power in Wallachia for a second reign, continuing efforts to strengthen autonomy.
Șerban, Constantin	1665-1669	Ruled Wallachia during a period of challenges and conflicts.
Leon, Radu	1669-1672	Served as voivode of Moldavia, but his reign was relatively short and faced difficulties.
Cantacuzino, Șerban	1672-1688	A Wallachian voivode known for both internal reforms and external conflicts.
Brâncoveanu, Constantin	1688-1714	Remembered for his cultural patronage, but his reign ended tragically with his execution by the Ottoman Empire.
Mavrocordatos, Nicholas	1714-1716	Served as voivode of Wallachia and worked towards stability in the region after years of conflict.
Cantacuzino, Ștefan	1716-1719	Another Wallachian voivode who faced political challenges during his rule.
Mavrocordatos, Nicholas (Second reign)	1719-1730	Returned to power for a second term as voivode of Wallachia.
Mavrocordatos, Constantin	1730-1737	A Wallachian ruler who worked on administrative and economic reforms.
Ghica, Grigore II	1733-1735	Served as voivode of Moldavia during a period of political manoeuvring.
Racoviță, Constantin	1735-1744	A voivode of Moldavia who faced various political challenges during his reign.

Name	Reign	Description
Mavrocordatos, Constantin (Second reign)	1744-1747	Returned to power for a second term as Wallachian voivode.
Mavrogheni, Nicolae	1744-1752	Served as Wallachia's voivode during a period of political and economic complexities.
Ghica, Scarlat	1752-1756	A Wallachian voivode whose reign faced various challenges.
Racoviță, Constantin (Second reign)	1756-1758	Returned to power for a second term as Moldavian voivode.
Lambrino, Alexandru	1758-1761	Served as Wallachian voivode during a period of political intrigue.
Ghica, Matei	1761-1764	A Wallachian ruler who faced challenges in maintaining order and stability.
Ghica, Grigore III	1764-1767	Served as voivode of Moldavia during a complex period in its history.
Ipsilanti, Alexandru	1768-1769	A Wallachian voivode who ruled during a short and turbulent period.
Racoviță, Mihai	1769-1770	Served as Moldavian voivode during a challenging period.
Callimachi, Alexandru	1770-1782	Served as both Wallachian and Moldavian voivode at different times and faced various political issues during his rule.
Ghica, Grigore IV (Second reign)	1782-1785	Returned to power for a second term as Wallachian voivode.
Muruzi, Alexandru	1785-1786	A Wallachian ruler whose reign was brief and marked by political challenges.
Callimachi, Alexandru (Second reign)	1786-1787	Returned to power for a second term as Moldavian voivode.
Callimachi, Scarlat	1787-1789	Served as voivode of Moldavia during a period of political unrest.
Caragea, Ioan George	1789-1790	Was a Wallachian voivode who faced challenges during his brief reign.
Caragea, Nicolae	1790-1792	Served as Moldavian voivode during a period of political and social change.
Muruzi, Alexandru (Second reign)	1792-1793	Returned to power for a second term as Wallachian voivode.
Hangerli, Constantin	1793-1797	Served as Wallachian voivode but faced challenges during his rule, including conflict with the Ottoman Empire.
Mourouzis, Alexander	1797-1801	Was a Wallachian voivode whose reign experienced political turmoil.

Soutzos, Alexander	1801-1802	Served as voivode of Wallachia but had a brief reign.
Mourouzis, George	1802-1806	A Wallachian ruler who faced internal and external challenges during his rule.
Ypsilantis, Constantine	1806-1807	Served as Wallachian voivode during a period of political unrest.
Soutzos, Alexander (Second reign)	1807-1808	Returned to power for a second term as Wallachian voivode.
Caradja, Jean Georges	1808-1812	Served as Wallachian voivode during a complex period marked by the Napoleonic Wars.
Ghica, Gregory IV (Second reign)	1812-1818	Returned to power for a second term as Wallachian voivode.
Caragea, Ioan Gheorghe	1818-1821	Returned to power for a second term as Wallachian voivode.
Soutzos, Alexander (Third reign)	1821-1822	Returned to power for a third term as Wallachian voivode.
Sturdza, John	1822-1828	A Moldavian ruler who worked on various reforms during his rule.
Caragea, Ioan Gheorghe (Second reign)	1828-1834	Returned to power for a second term as Wallachian voivode.
Ghica, Alexandru II	1834-1842	A Wallachian ruler known for his efforts to modernize the principality.
Sturdza, Michael	1834-1849	Served as Moldavian ruler and continued reforms in Moldavia.
Ştirbei, Barbu Dimitrie	1849-1856	A Wallachian ruler who worked on various reforms and modernization efforts.
Cuza, Alexander John	1859-1866	Became the ruler of the United Principalities of Moldavia and Wallachia, a precursor to modern Romania.

RULERS/LEADERS DURING ROMANIA'S MODERN PERIOD

Ruler/Leader	Date	Notes
Cuza, Alexandru Ioan	1859-1866	The first ruler of the United Principalities of Moldavia and Wallachia, which later became the basis for modern Romania.
Carol I	1866-1914	The first king of Romania from 1881 when Romania became a kingdom until his death in 1914. His reign saw significant modernization and expansion of the Romanian state.
Ferdinand I	1914-1927	Succeeded Carol I and reigned during World War I. His reign was marked by Romania's entry into the war on the side of the Allies in 1916.
Michael I	1927-1930	Served as king twice, with his first reign being a brief period as a child. His second reign began during World War II and continued until he was forced to abdicate by the Communist government in 1955.
Antonescu, Ion	1940-1944	As a military dictator and Prime Minister, Ion Antonescu led Romania during its alliance with Nazi Germany in World War II. His leadership ended with Romania switching sides to the Allies in 1944.
Groza, Petru	1945-1952	Romania's first Communist Prime Minister, he played a significant role in the early years of the Communist regime.
Gheorghiu-Dej, Gheorghe	1947-1965	The General Secretary of the Romanian Workers' Party who later became the President of the State Council, effectively the leader of Communist Romania.
Ceaușescu, Nicolae	1965-1989	One of the most prominent Communist leaders in Romania's history, serving as General Secretary of the Romanian Communist Party and President of Romania until he was overthrown and executed during the Romanian Revolution in 1989.
Iliescu, Ion	1989-1996, 2000-2004	A key figure in the post-Communist transition period, serving as President of Romania in two non-consecutive terms.
Băsescu, Traian	2004-2014	Served as Romania's President for two terms during a period of political/economic reform.
Iohannis, Klaus	2014-to date	The President of Romania, elected in 2014 and re-elected in 2019, and remains a key figure in modern Romanian politics.

PRIME MINISTERS OF ROMANIA

Prime Minister	Dates	Notes
Roman, Petre	Dec 26, 1989 – Oct 19, 1991	Played a key role in the early days of the transition.
Stolojan, Theodor	Oct 19, 1991 – Nov 19, 1992	Served during a period of economic challenges.
Văcăroiu, Nicolae	Nov 19, 1992 – Dec 12, 1996	Led a government during a period of political change and economic reform.
Ciorbea, Victor	Dec 12, 1996 – Mar 30, 1998	Faced challenges during his tenure - protests and political instability.
Vasile, Radu	Mar 30, 1998 – Dec 17, 1999	Served during a time when Romania was seeking closer ties with Western institutions.
Isărescu, Mugur	Dec 17, 1999 – Dec 28, 2000	An economist, was appointed as Prime Minister during a financial crisis.
Năstase, Adrian	Dec 28, 2000 – Dec 4, 2004	A prominent political figure who served during Romania's path towards EU accession.
Popescu-Tăriceanu, Călin	Dec 29, 2004 – Dec 22, 2008	Focused on economic and administrative reforms.
Boc, Emil	Dec 22, 2008 – Feb 6, 2012	Served non-consecutive terms, dealing with economic challenges and social protests
Ponta, Victor	Dec 21, 2012 – Nov 4, 2015	His tenure saw political controversies and protests.
Cioloș, Dacian	Nov 17, 2015 – Jan 4, 2017	An independent technocrat appointed to lead a government focused on reforms.
Grindeanu, Sorin	Jan 4, 2017 – Jun 21, 2017	Served a short term as Prime Minister.
Tudose, Mihai	Jun 29, 2017 – Jan 29, 2018	Faced political challenges during his tenure.
Dăncilă, Viorica	Jan 29, 2018 – Nov 4, 2019	Romania's first female Prime Minister.
Orban, Ludovic	Nov 4, 2019 – Dec 7, 2020	Led Romania through political and health challenges, including the COVID-19 pandemic.
Ciucă, Nicolae	Dec 7, 2020 – Dec 23, 2020	Short-term acting Prime Minister
Cîțu, Florin	Dec 23, 2020 – Nov 25, 2021	Between Sep 2021 and Apr 2022, he was also the leader of the National Liberal Party (PNL).
Ciucă, Nicolae Lonel	Nov 7, 2021 - Jun 12, 2023	A retired general of the Romanian Land Forces, who is now currently serving as the President of the Senate of Romania. His ideology is conservative based.
Cătălin, Marian Predoiu	Jun 12, 2023 - Jun 15, 2023	A lawyer who served as an interim Prime Minister.
Ciolacu, Ion-Marcel	Jun 15, 2023 - to date	He currently serves as the Prime Minister and is also the leader of the Social Democratic Party (PSD).

INDEX

IMAGE CREDITS

Title	Citation
Thracians	(2023, September 6). In Wikipedia. https://en.wikipedia.org/wiki/Thracians
King Burebista Emperor Aurelian	(2023, September 2). In Wikipedia. https://en.wikipedia.org/wiki/Burebista
Peștera cu Oase	(2023, June 12). In Wikipedia. https://en.wikipedia.org/wiki/Pe%C8%99tera_cu_Oase
Roman Dacia	(2023, September 6). In Wikipedia. https://en.wikipedia.org/wiki/Roman_Dacia
Emperor Aurelian	(2023, September 2). In Wikipedia. https://en.wikipedia.org/wiki/Aurelian
Stephen the Great	(2023, September 4). In Wikipedia. https://en.wikipedia.org/wiki/Stephen_the_Great
Alexandru Ioan Cuza	(2023, August 5). In Wikipedia. https://ro.wikipedia.org/wiki/Alexandru_Ioan_Cuza
Ottoman Empire 1875	(2023, September 5). In Wikipedia. https://en.wikipedia.org/wiki/Ottoman_Empire
Michael the Brave (Mihai Viteazu)	(2023, August 23). In Wikipedia. https://en.wikipedia.org/wiki/Michael_the_Brave
Ottoman v Phanariotes (Bucharest)	(2023, July 2). In Wikipedia. https://en.wikipedia.org/wiki/Greeks_in_Romania
Mihai Eminescu	(2023, September 3). In *Wikipedia*. https://en.wikipedia.org/wiki/Mihai_Eminescu
King Carol I	(2023, August 21). In Wikipedia. https://en.wikipedia.org/wiki/Carol_I_of_Romania
United Romania 1862	(2023, August 8). In Wikipedia. https://en.wikipedia.org/wiki/Alexandru_Ioan_Cuza
Signing The Treaty of San Stefano 1878	(2023, August 24). In Wikipedia. https://en.wikipedia.org/wiki/Treaty_of_San_Stefano
The Declaration of The Kingdom of Romania	(2023, September 2). In Wikipedia. https://en.wikipedia.org/wiki/Kingdom_of_Romania
Romanian Troops at Mărășești in 1917	(2023, September 2). In Wikipedia. https://en.wikipedia.org/wiki/Romania_in_World_War_I
Kingdom of Romania 1918 – 1940	(2023, June 18). In Wikipedia. https://en.wikipedia.org/wiki/Greater_Romania
Michael I of Romania	(2023, September 9). In *Wikipedia*. https://en.wikipedia.org/wiki/Michael_I_of_Romania
Petru Groza	(2023, September 6). In Wikipedia. https://en.wikipedia.org/wiki/Petru_Groza
Nicolae Ceaușescu	(2023, September 7). In Wikipedia. https://en.wikipedia.org/wiki/Nicolae_Ceau%C8%99escu
The 1989 Revolution - Bucharest	(2023, August 31). In Wikipedia. https://en.wikipedia.org/wiki/Romanian_revolution
Ludovic Orban	(2023, June 5). In *Wikipedia*. https://en.wikipedia.org/wiki/Ludovic_Orban
Author Mircea Cărtărescu.	(2023, August 31). In *Wikipedia*. https://en.wikipedia.org/wiki/Mircea_C%C4%83rt%C4%83rescu
Bucharest – Romania's Capital	Romania. (2023, September 5). In *Wikipedia*. https://en.wikipedia.org/wiki/Romania

ABOUT THE AUTHOR

Martin Miller-Yianni, a London native born in 1958, hails from a humble working-class background. Although he initially pursued a career as a primary school teacher, his life took an unexpected turn when he ventured into Eastern Europe in 2005.

Since his arrival, Martin has fully embraced the unique way of life and culture, igniting a passion for writing within him. Having served as a journalist and researcher for a leading information website about Eastern Europe, he has developed a profound knowledge, understanding, and first-hand experience of this part of the world.

Martin's connection with the region continues to inspire and influence his literary endeavours.

OTHER BOOKS BY THE AUTHOR

365 Bulgarian Adventures
(2006)
Publication Pending

26 Tales of Humanities Trials
(2023)
ISBN 978-619-92494-8-2

Simple Treasures in Bulgaria
(2008)
ISBN 978-0-9559-8490-7

I'm Bad at Poems
(2022)
ISBN 978-619-92494-2-0

Bulgaria Through the Ages
(2010)
ISBN 978-1-4476-2777-7

Redemption of Love
(2023)
ISBN 978-619-92494-0-6

100 Essential Recipes from Bulgaria
(2011)
ISBN 978-1-4477-0260-3

2-Mile Open Water Swim with Hurdles
(2020)
ISBN 978-619-91520-1-0